My First Communion

Memory Book

This book belongs to

Place your photo here

All About Me

Full name

Date of birth

Baptism date

Parents' names

Godparents' names

Parish name

My Ceremony

First Holy Communion date

Church

Time of service

Officiant

Who attended

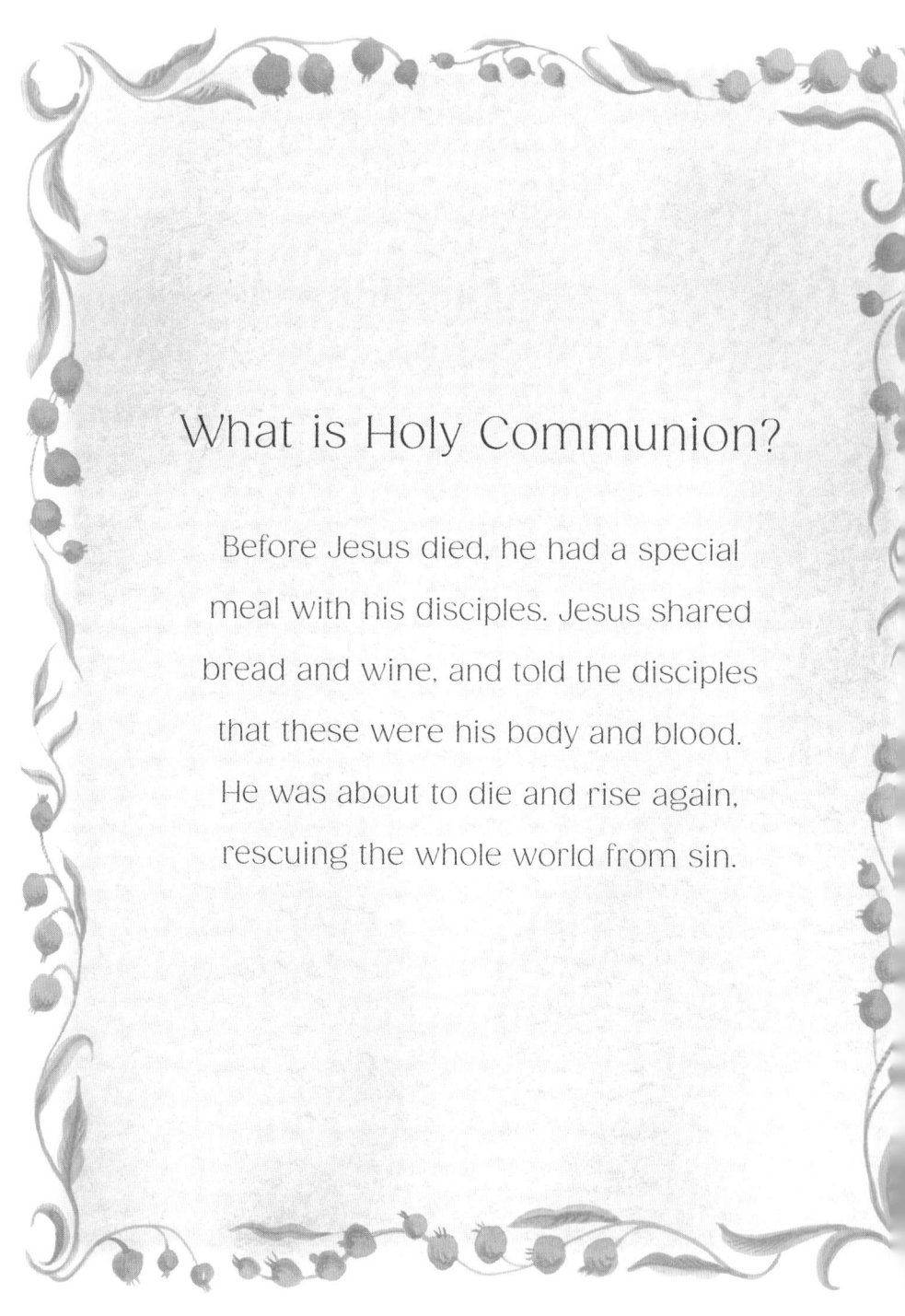

What is Holy Communion?

Before Jesus died, he had a special meal with his disciples. Jesus shared bread and wine, and told the disciples that these were his body and blood. He was about to die and rise again, rescuing the whole world from sin.

He asked his friends to keep sharing bread and wine to remember this, and today, we call this Holy Communion. When we share it, we remember Jesus' sacrifice; we know that we are joined with him and all Christians everywhere; and we look forward to the kingdom of heaven.

My Special Day

Place your photo here

Place your photo here

"'Lord, I'm not worthy for you to come under my roof.

Just say the word, and my servant will be healed.'"

(Matthew 8:8)

Journal your faith journey

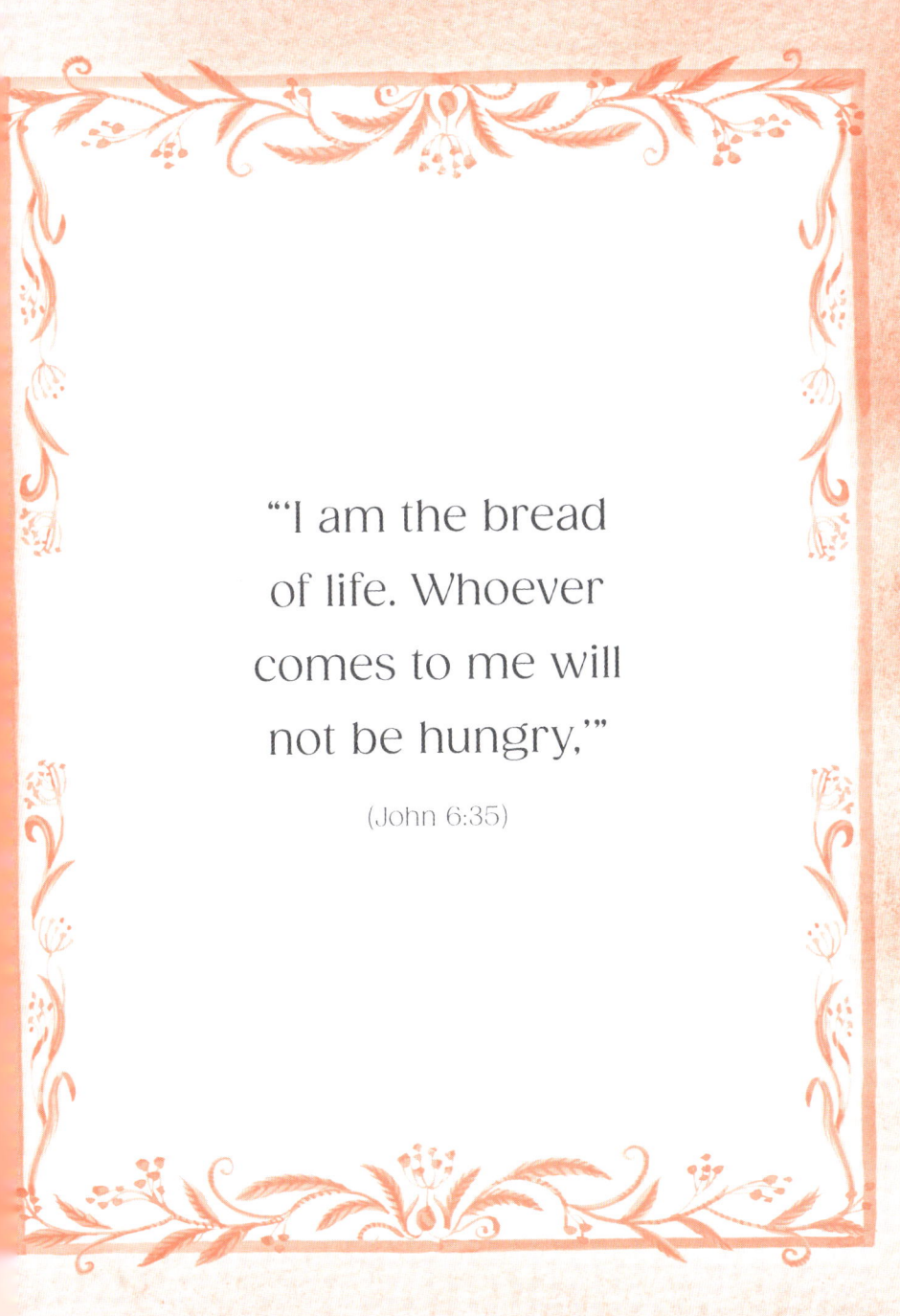

"'I am the bread of life. Whoever comes to me will not be hungry,'"

(John 6:35)

Everyone who took communion with me

My First Holy Communion

Place your photo here

Place your photo here

My Holy Communion Outfit

Place your photo here

Place your photo here

Hymns that we sang

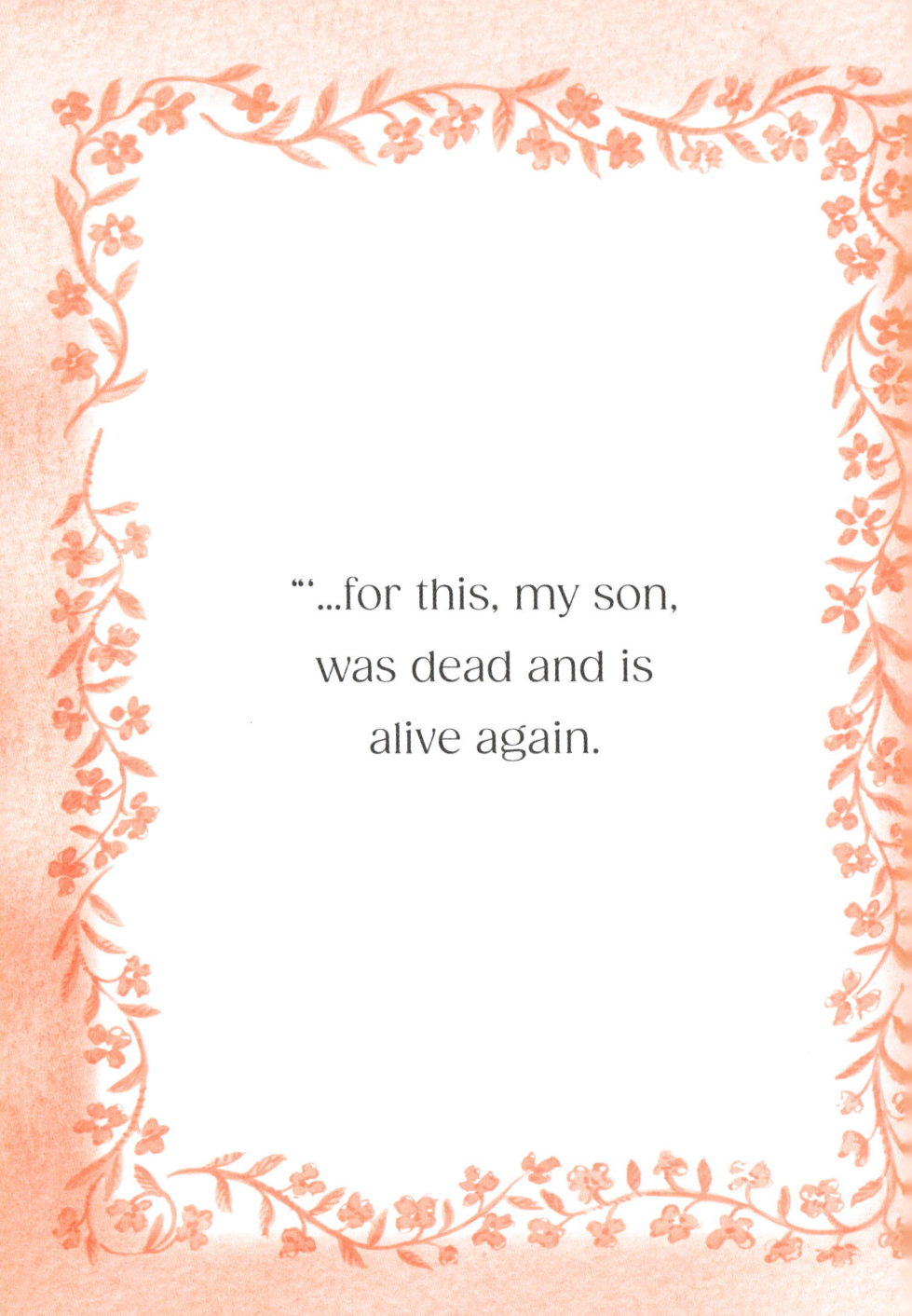

"'...for this, my son, was dead and is alive again.

He was lost and
is found.'"

(Luke 15:24)

Act of Spiritual Communion

This is a prayer to say when you're unable to attend Communion.

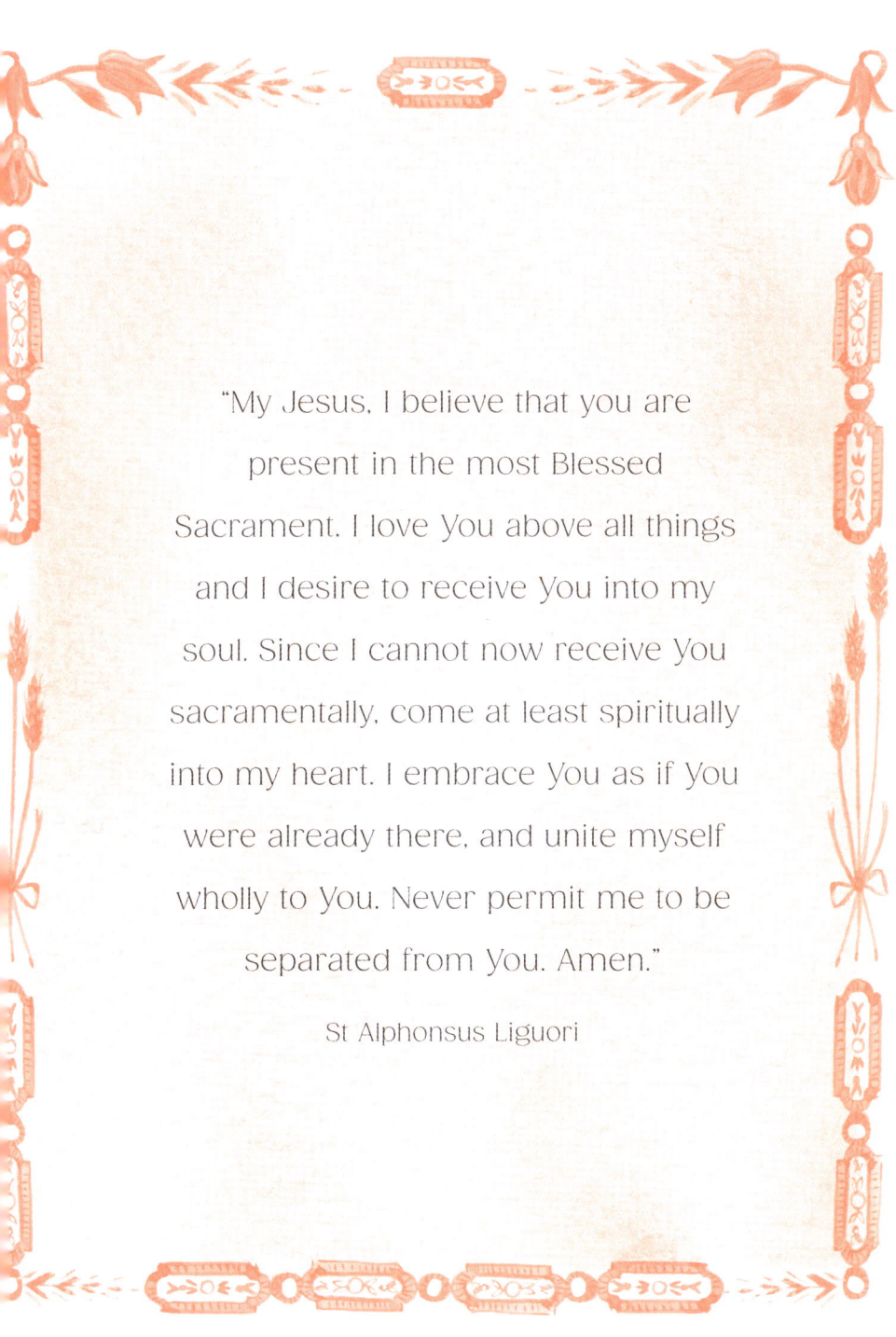

"My Jesus, I believe that you are present in the most Blessed Sacrament. I love You above all things and I desire to receive You into my soul. Since I cannot now receive You sacramentally, come at least spiritually into my heart. I embrace You as if You were already there, and unite myself wholly to You. Never permit me to be separated from You. Amen."

St Alphonsus Liguori

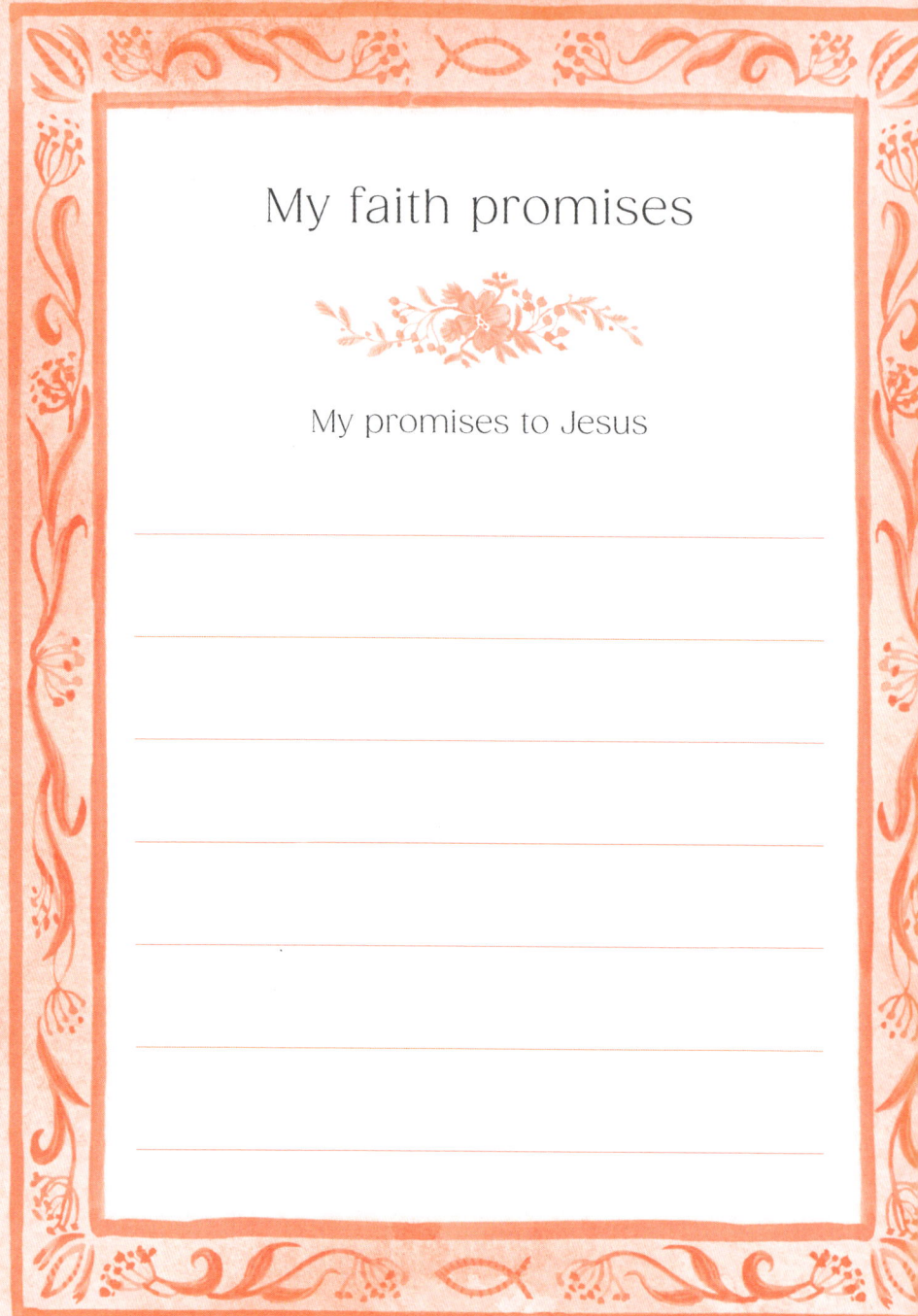

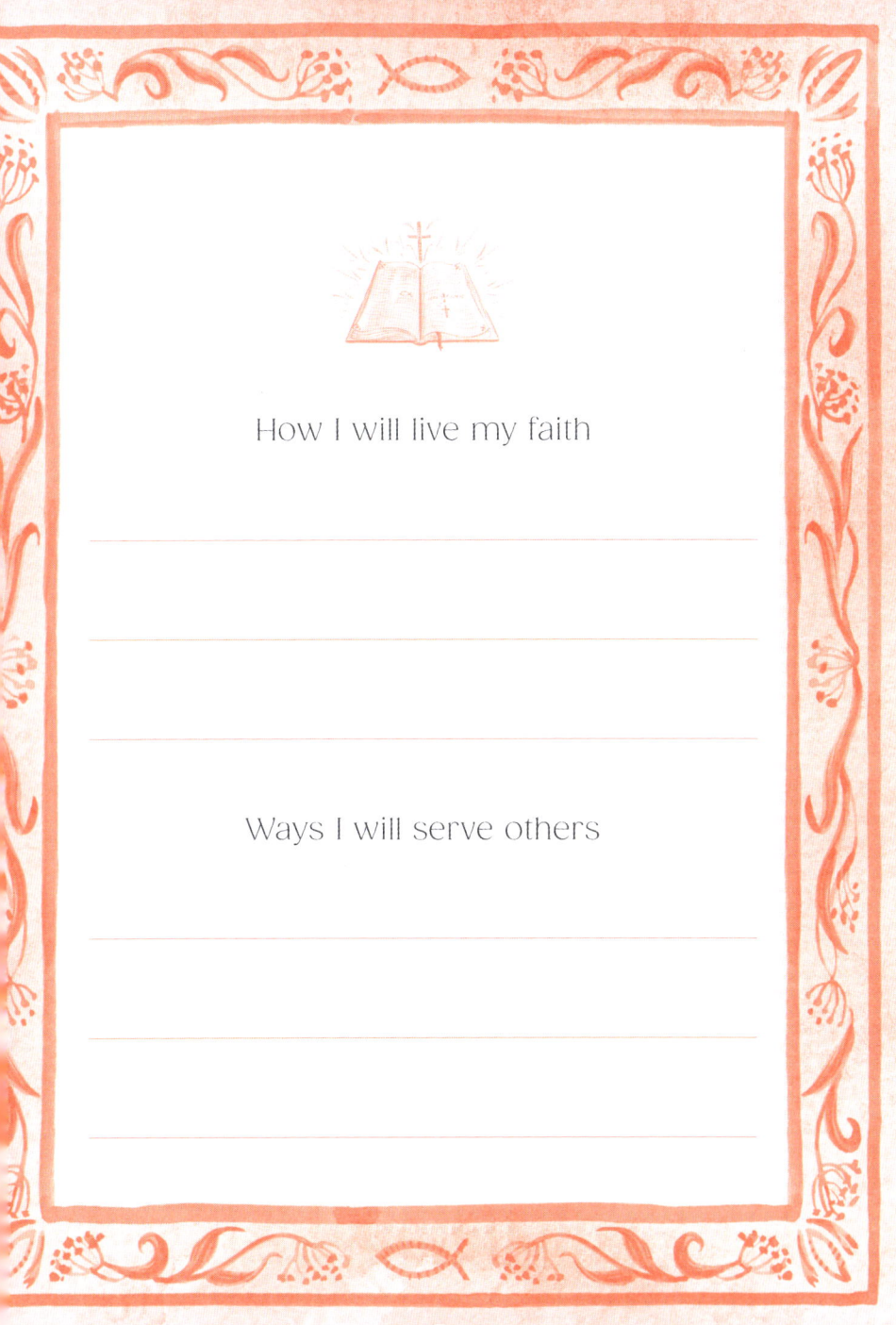

How I will live my faith

Ways I will serve others

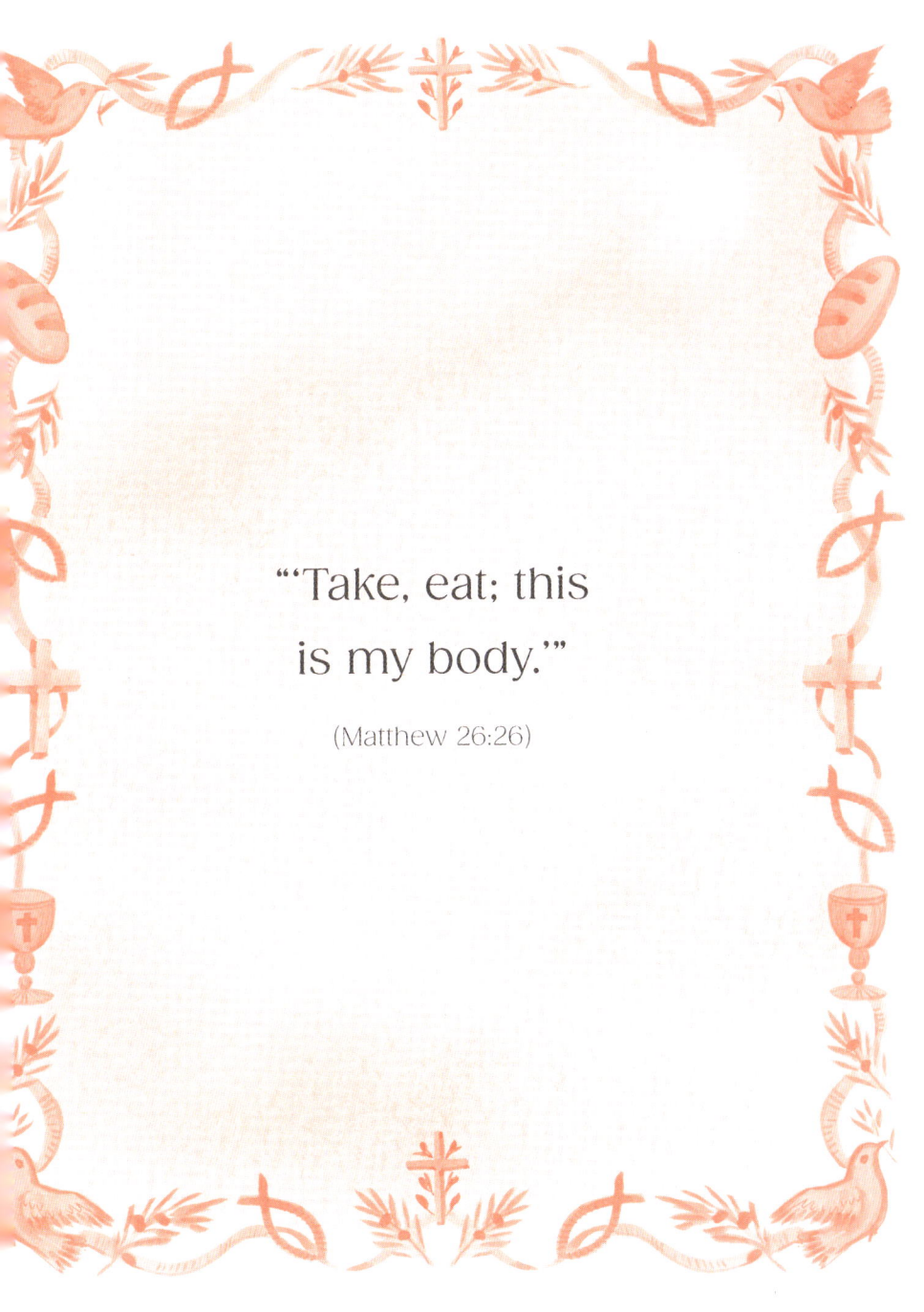

"'Take, eat; this is my body.'"

(Matthew 26:26)

What is a Saint?

A saint is a person who has done their very best to follow Jesus and to do what he says. No human being has ever been perfect apart from Jesus. But the saints are examples of how a person who is close to Jesus can lead a life that builds the kingdom of heaven.

Hebrews 12:1 talks about a "great cloud of witnesses" that cheers us on in our own life of faith. They are the Communion of Saints who are now with God in heaven – not because they led perfect lives, but because they believed in Jesus and were saved by his death and resurrection.

My saint's prayer

Gifts given to me on my special day

The Prayer of St Richard of Chichester

Thanks be to thee, my Lord Jesus Christ, for all the benefits thou hast given me, for all the pains and insults thou hast borne for me.

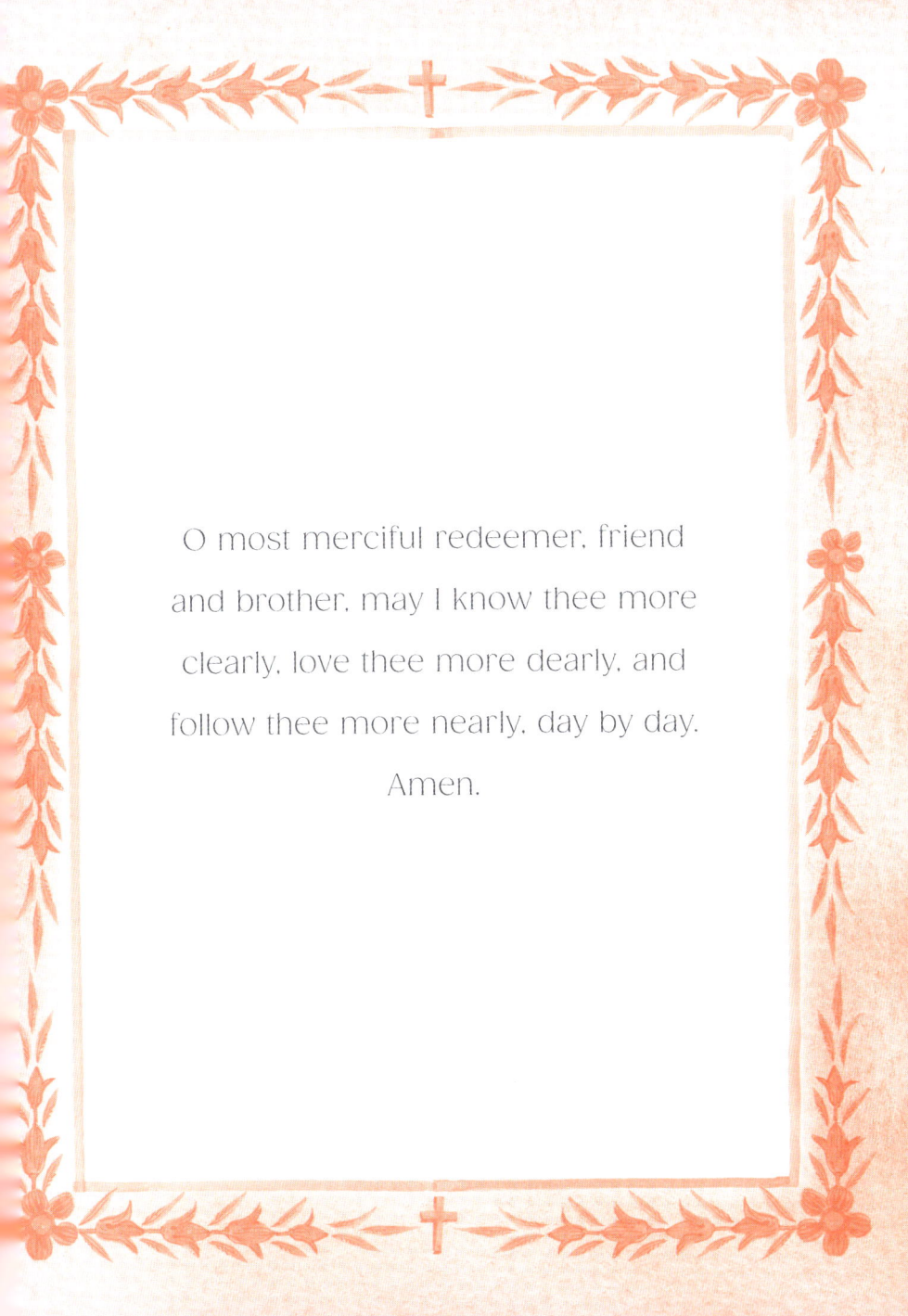

O most merciful redeemer, friend and brother, may I know thee more clearly, love thee more dearly, and follow thee more nearly, day by day. Amen.

A moment of reflection

The most special moment of my day

How I felt taking communion

Memories to cherish

My continued faith journey

My future sacraments

My future religious education

My spiritual goals

A letter for the future

A letter for the future

"'Do this in memory of me.'"

(Luke 22:19)

Thoughts, hopes, and messages

from those who matter most

Thoughts, hopes, and messages

from those who matter most

Thoughts, hopes, and messages

from those who matter most

Thoughts, hopes, and messages

from those who matter most

Thoughts, hopes, and messages

from those who matter most

Thoughts, hopes, and messages

from those who matter most

Thoughts, hopes, and messages

from those who matter most

Thoughts, hopes, and messages

from those who matter most

Thoughts, hopes, and messages

from those who matter most

Thoughts, hopes, and messages

from those who matter most

Place your photo here

Place your photo here

Place your photo here

Place your photo here

Place your photo here

Place your photo here

Place your photo here

Illustrated by Victoria Nelson

First published in Great Britain in 2026 by
Dorling Kindersley Limited
20 Vauxhall Bridge Road,
London SW1V 2SA

The authorised representative in the EEA is
Dorling Kindersley Verlag GmbH. Arnulfstr. 124,
80636 Munich, Germany

Copyright © 2026 Dorling Kindersley Limited
A Penguin Random House Company
10 9 8 7 6 5 4 3 2 1
001–352581–Mar/2026

All Scripture quotations are taken from
the World English Bible (WEB)

All rights reserved.
No part of this publication may be reproduced, stored
in or introduced into a retrieval system, or transmitted,
in any form, or by any means (electronic, mechanical,
photocopying, recording, or otherwise), without the
prior written permission of the copyright owner.
No part of this publication may be used or reproduced in
any manner for the purpose of training artificial intelligence
technologies or systems. In accordance with Article 4(3)
of the DSM Directive 2019/790, DK expressly reserves
this work from the text and data mining exception.

A CIP catalogue record for this book
is available from the British Library.
ISBN: 978-0-2417-7111-2

Printed and bound in India

www.dk.com

This book was made with Forest Stewardship Council™ certified paper – one small step in DK's commitment to a sustainable future.
Learn more at www.dk.com/uk/information/sustainability